TRAVEL
HACKS

TRAVEL
HACKS

**Any Procedures or Actions That Solve a Problem,
Simplify a Task, Reduce Frustration, and Make
Your Next Trip As Awesome As Possible**

KEITH BRADFORD
Author of *Life Hacks*

Adams Media
New York   London   Toronto   Sydney   New Delhi

A adamsmedia

Adams Media
An Imprint of Simon & Schuster, Inc.
100 Technology Center Drive
Stoughton, Massachusetts 02072

First Adams Media trade
paperback edition September 2021

ADAMS MEDIA and colophon are
trademarks of Simon & Schuster.

For information about special
discounts for bulk purchases,
please contact Simon & Schuster
Special Sales at 1-866-506-1949 or
business@simonandschuster.com.

The Simon & Schuster Speakers
Bureau can bring authors to your
live event. For more information
or to book an event contact the
Simon & Schuster Speakers Bureau
at 1-866-248-3049 or visit our
website at www.simonspeakers.com.

Interior design by Julia Jacintho
Interior illustrations by Kathy Konkle
and Priscilla Yuen
Interior images © 123RF/1enchik,
Aleksandra Alekseeva, Denys
Kryvyi, natashapankina, rastudio

Manufactured in the United States
of America

1 2021

Library of Congress Cataloging-in-
Publication Data
Names: Bradford, Keith, author.
Title: Travel hacks / Keith Bradford,
author of Life Hacks.
Description: First Adams Media
Trade Paperback Edition. | Avon,
Massachusetts: Adams Media, 2021.
Series: Hacks. | Includes index.
Identifiers: LCCN 2020003849 |
ISBN 9781507213520 (pb) |
ISBN 9781507213537 (ebook)
Subjects: LCSH: Travel--Miscellanea. |
Consumer education--Miscellanea. |
Life skills--Miscellanea.
Classification: LCC G151 .B685 2020 |
DDC 910.2/02--dc23
LC record available at https://lccn
.loc.gov/2020003849

ISBN 978-1-5072-1352-0
ISBN 978-1-5072-1353-7 (ebook)

CONTENTS

INTRODUCTION

Flight delays, traffic jams, lost luggage. Traveling, whether it's down the street or across the world, can often be hectic, stressful, and expensive. Well, not to worry—*Travel Hacks* is here to help!

In these pages, we've collected more than six hundred quick and easy hacks to help you simplify the traveling experience, so you can get where you need to be without all the headaches and hidden costs burning a hole in your pocket. We've gathered secret tips, shortcuts, and detailed lists to prepare you for your journey, help you survive air travel, maximize your vacations, and get back home safe and sound.

The hacks in this book are broken down into chapters centered on certain themes, like planning and booking, packing smart, traveling with kids, and road tripping, to help get you through any vacation, commute, or work trip. You can read the section where you need the most help, or just flip to any page for a quick travel fix. Whatever you need help with, we've got you covered, so turn to any page and learn to travel like a pro!

Chapter 1

PLANNING AND BOOKING

1

Planning on doing a three-day weekend trip? Take Monday off instead of Friday. It's generally much cheaper to fly Saturday to Monday than to fly Friday to Sunday.

2

Tuesdays at 3:00 p.m., six weeks before your flight, has been proven to be the absolute cheapest time your tickets will ever be.

3

Compared to late-night flights, early morning flights tend to be less crowded and have a lower chance of being delayed on takeoff or landing.

4

To determine how much you'll spend on a trip, research how much bread, beer, and milk cost in your destination country—it's the best way to get a sense of how expensive somewhere is.

5

Try using a PC rather than a Mac when exploring hotel booking websites. These websites can tell what type of computer you are using and will show Mac users more expensive bookings first. According to *The Wall Street Journal*, Mac users are charged $20 to $30 more.

6

If you're looking for cheap flights during the holiday season, your first instinct may be to look at coach class tickets, but actually many business and economy-plus seats are cheaper at this time. This is because there are a lot more general travelers and a lot fewer business travelers during this time of year.

7

Before leaving for a work trip, look over your company's expense policy. You might discover that you can expense things you never thought about, like sunscreen.

8

Checking up on flight departure times? Rather than sift through the local airport's website, simply type the airline and flight number into Google search to get all the up-to-date information you need.

9

When booking a flight that has a layover through the United States, keep in mind that the minimum time you'll need for a layover is an hour and a half. Anything less and there's a good chance you won't be able to catch the next flight.

10

Can't decide where to go on vacation? Flip a coin—not to decide for you, but because you'll realize what you really want when it's in the air.

11

LOOKING TO WORK SOMEWHERE ABROAD? THE EASIEST PLACES FOR PEOPLE FROM NORTH AMERICA, SOUTH AMERICA, EUROPE, AND ASIA TO GO WORK ARE NEW ZEALAND AND AUSTRALIA. BOTH COUNTRIES OFFER A VISA CALLED THE "WORKING HOLIDAY" VISA, WHICH ALLOWS YOU TO WORK IN ANY UNSKILLED/ MINIMALLY SKILLED JOB FOR UP TO A YEAR.

12

Can't find a cheap flight to your destination?
Try searching for two one-way tickets. Your
journey might have a longer layover, and it
might be more of a hassle, but it can be worth
the amount of money you could save.

13

Hate paying those excess baggage fees at the
airport? Check the airline's website to find out
how much you're allowed to bring and then weigh
your suitcases on a mini-luggage scale before
leaving. A scale is only about $15 to $20 online
but can save you hundreds in extra bagging fees.

14

Check out exchange rates at places in the country
you're going to. Sometimes it can be cheaper
to exchange money at your bank before you
leave, and in some cases it's even cheaper to
take money out of an ATM when you get there.

15

Planning a trip to another country? Get some simple tips on what to bring, where to eat, what to pack, and so on by doing an online search for "things I wish I knew before visiting (country)."

16

Before flying internationally, make sure to take down the contact info and location for your country's embassy in the destination country.

17

Before reading a travel website's tips for things to do, take a quick look at your own city's tips to get an idea of the kinds of things they'll be recommending.

18

The "skiplagged" method helps you get to your destination cheaper as the layover, and not the final destination. For example, a New York to Orlando flight is $250, but a flight from New York to Austin with a layover in Orlando is $150. You can search for these deals at *Skiplagged*.

19

If you end up booking a skiplagged flight and it gets canceled (about 2.5 percent do), the airline is not obligated to get you to the middle destination. Although 97.5 percent of the time you'll be okay, keep this in mind.

20

Before traveling overseas, make sure to check your passport's expiration date. Some countries don't accept passports that are set to expire within six months. So even if you have a valid passport, it might not be accepted.

21

If you're going to a new town and don't know what to do there, call a local hotel, say you're staying there next week, and ask any question you want.

22

Always make sure to book your seat as close to the back of the plane as possible. Studies have shown this is where the most plane crash survivors have been seated.

23

Don't want to pay Walgreens or CVS $15 for a passport photo? Go to www.travel.state .gov (owned by the US government) and use their tool to crop and make your own.

24

In general, when buying airline tickets online, fourteen days before your departure date is when the most significant price increases happen.

25

THE PRICES FOR FLIGHTS
ACTUALLY GO UP THE MORE
TIMES YOU VISIT A SITE,
SO USE YOUR BROWSER'S
INCOGNITO TAB OR DELETE
YOUR BROWSER'S HISTORY
EVERY TIME YOU CHECK
FLIGHT RATES. RATES
CAN ALSO CHANGE UP TO
THREE TIMES PER DAY.

26

Constantly worrying about losing your passport? There are several tracking devices you can purchase for your wallet or passport that allow you to track them if they ever get misplaced.

27

If your traveling dates are not set in stone, try searching for tickets at *momondo*. They'll show you the price differences on dates surrounding your selection. Simply staying or leaving one extra day could save you a few hundred dollars.

28

Before committing to a hotel or apartment, check out the *Bedbug Registry* (https://bedbugregistry.com/search/) or *Bedbug Reports* (www.bedbugreports.com). These websites will show you hotels around the world where bedbugs have been reported.

29

Worried you're not going to get the cheapest hotel possible? Try booking through *AllTheRooms* (www.alltherooms.com). They'll search all the discount hotel sites, plus *Airbnb*, *VRBO*, *Couchsurfing*, and more.

30

If you're one to get a bad case of stomach turbulence, book a seat as close to the wing of the plane as possible. There is much more stability at this part of the plane.

31

Want some free bonus frequent flyer points? Various credit cards have promotions that will give you 100,000 plus points just for applying. Just make sure you're the kind of person who pays off your credit card balances on time.

32

When applying for a travel visa, always go to that country's official government website. There are lots of other sites that may have the ability to get you one, but they will charge you ten times more. These "scam" sites are often at the top of an Internet search and are labeled "ad."

33

You can save some of the money you'd spend on a hotel by booking those long train or bus trips to be overnight.

34

Typically, the time to book the cheapest flights is six to eight weeks before you want to travel.

35

Tuesday and Wednesday are the days to buy the least expensive tickets. The cheapest days to fly out on are Tuesday, Wednesday, and Saturday.

36

Booking a cruise? Book a room in the lower-level cabins near the center of the ship. You may not get an ocean view, but it is less likely you'll experience motion sickness.

37

One of the least expensive ways to travel is to stay at hostels, but it can be hard to find the right ones. *Hostelworld* will show you all the hostels in your desired area, along with ratings, reviews, contact information, and prices.

38

By using online shopping reward sites, like *Evreward* (https://evreward.com) and *CashbackMonitor* (www.cashbackmonitor.com), you can see deals for everyday items that offer bonus extra frequent flyer points.

39

THE BEST TIMES TO TRAVEL
ARE DURING SHOULDER
SEASONS, MONSOON
SEASONS, RAINY SEASONS,
AND HOT SEASONS,
AS THERE WILL BE FAR
FEWER TOURISTS, AND
YOU WILL GET A MORE
REALISTIC LOOK AT YOUR
DESTINATION. IT'S ALSO
MUCH CHEAPER TO TRAVEL
DURING THESE SEASONS.

40

Want to get away for the weekend but don't want the hassle of doing all the booking/planning? Let a surprise travel-planning agency, like *Pack Up + Go* (www.packupgo.com), do everything for you. They'll book your flight, accommodations, and even pick your destination.

41

Always try running multiple departure dates when booking your tickets online. By leaving a day early or staying an extra day you can save a couple of hundred dollars on your flight.

42

If you are a US citizen and book a flight, you should be aware that you can get a full refund within twenty-four hours, no questions asked. This is the law, and it even applies to foreign airlines if you mention you are from the United States.

43

Don't have the money to travel? There's a program called WWOOF (Worldwide Opportunities on Organic Farms) at https://wwoof.net, which will connect you to farms and other places abroad that need volunteer work in exchange for food and a place to stay.

44

If you're using a travel agent, ask about deals on excursions, entertainment, and other perks. Agents often have discounts and connections that online booking sites don't offer.

45

Planning on bringing back a bunch of souvenirs? Stuff an extra duffel bag in your suitcase. They fold over easily to take up little space, and you can just swing it over your shoulder once it's filled with goodies.

46

Most people think the earlier the better when it comes to buying airline tickets. This is not the case. Booking too early (six months out) can actually result in paying up to 19 percent more for your tickets.

47

Some car insurance companies allow you to pause and unease your policy. For longer trips, this can help you save a few hundred dollars just by making one phone call.

48

Empty your sink and dishwasher before you leave. No one wants to come home to dirty dishes that may be growing mold or a stinky dishwasher, so do yourself a favor and leave them clean.

49

RIGHT BEFORE YOU LEAVE, TAKE A PICTURE OF YOUR STOVE. IF YOU PANIC LATER ABOUT WHETHER OR NOT YOU TURNED OFF ALL THE BURNERS, YOUR PHOTOS WILL PROVIDE VISUAL PROOF THAT YOU DID. THIS METHOD ALSO WORKS FOR CONFIRMING THAT YOU'VE CLOSED YOUR WINDOWS OR DONE ANYTHING ELSE YOU ARE PRONE TO WORRY ABOUT.

Chapter 2

PACKING
SMART

50

You can make any backpack or suitcase waterproof by rubbing a coating of beeswax over the outside area.

51

Before you close up your suitcase, throw in a dryer sheet. Your clothes will smell like they just got out of the dryer when you get to your destination; plus, the dryer sheet will reduce static.

52

Make sure to cover your razor heads before putting them in your suitcase. Any binder clip works perfectly for this job.

53

Don't want your work shirts to rip or wrinkle while you're traveling? Pop them in a plastic file folder. Plus, this makes them super easy to pack.

54

WHEN TAGGING YOUR
LUGGAGE WITH YOUR NAME,
CONTACT INFO, AND SO ON,
MAKE SURE TO PUT A TAG
ON THE INSIDE TOO. TAGS
ON THE OUTSIDE CAN FALL
OFF OR BE REMOVED, BUT
IF YOUR BAG GETS LOST,
THE AIRLINE WILL OPEN IT
UP TO TRY TO DETERMINE
WHO IT BELONGS TO.

55

Whenever you make a packing list for a trip, make two copies, and pack the second one to make sure you bring everything back.

56

Before closing your suitcase, grab a fresh T-shirt, underwear, and socks and put them in your carry-on. If your luggage gets lost, at least you have a fresh change of clothes after your travels.

57

Try to avoid packing a deck of cards in your carry-on luggage, as it will light up on x-rays and become a "red flag" for TSA.

58

Take note that when budget airlines say they allow only one onboard personal item, they don't count pillows. You can even stuff a few items of clothing in the case and get away with it.

59

Puffy jackets or winter wear taking up too much room in your suitcase? Pack them in a compression bag. These bags can shrink puffy items down to about 25 percent of their normal size, and they don't require a vacuum (which may help out on the way home).

60

When packing your backpack, always try to distribute the weight so that your heaviest items are in the middle, closest to your back. This will give you better balance and put less strain on your back.

61

Giving a speech or presentation at your destination? Always keep a backup copy separate from your laptop, either on a USB in your carry-on bag or somewhere you can access it online.

62

When you pack for a backpacking trip, always make sure to roll your clothes. You can fit almost twice as much by doing this, and it also prevents creases.

63

Most airlines are pretty good at tracking missing luggage, but they're not the greatest at keeping you updated about its status. If you're worried about this, you can throw a luggage tracker in your suitcase. These allow you to track your suitcase in real time anywhere in the world.

64

Always make sure to take a quick photo of your suitcase before traveling. This will help speed up the paperwork process if you ever lose your luggage.

65

Save some space in your suitcase by tossing small things like socks, underwear, toiletries, and so on, inside your shoes.

66

Mark your luggage or backpack as "Fragile." Not only will people handle it with more care; the fragile items are usually stored at the top of the pile, meaning you'll get your bags back first.

67

Transfer your perfume, cologne, or aftershave into a plastic spray-top bottle. It can save space and eliminate the risk of the bottle breaking in your travel bag.

68

Traveling with jewelry? Pill containers make for a safe and convenient organizer.

69

CUT DOWN ON TOILETRIES
BY BRINGING JUST HAIR
CONDITIONER. THIS CAN
BE USED FOR A VARIETY OF
THINGS, INCLUDING SHAVING
FOAM, STYLING CREAM/
HAIR GEL, EYE MAKEUP
REMOVER, CUTICLE CREAM,
AND LAUNDRY DETERGENT. IT
CAN ALSO ACT AS SUNSCREEN
FOR YOUR HAIR IF YOU COMB
A LITTLE BIT IN BEFORE GOING
TO THE POOL OR THE BEACH.

70

If you're planning on traveling with locals or backpacking alone, bring a few small souvenirs from home to give out as thanks. They also make great conversation starters.

71

Never get your dirty and clean clothes mixed up again; simply turn your dirty clothes inside out after wearing them.

72

Let this be a warning: Whatever amount of socks you think you'll need, add 50 percent to it.

73

Sick of your hat getting crushed in your suitcase? Fold up a shirt and stuff it inside the hat. No more squishy hat!

74

Before packing up your makeup bag, throw some cotton pads or balls inside each makeup compact. This will stop powder makeup from breaking apart in your suitcase or bag.

75

Want to make sure the clothes in your suitcase or backpack stay dry? Line the inside with a few garbage bags.

76

Those tiny paint roller covers are perfect for holding your rings securely and keeping them scratch-free during your travels.

How to Efficiently Pack a Suitcase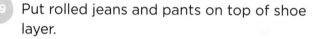

77 Roll your clothing tightly.

78 Place your heavier items like shoes at the four corners and walls.

79 Put rolled jeans and pants on top of shoe layer.

80 Lighter items like sweaters and shorts go in next.

81 Shirts and delicates that cannot be rolled go on next.

82 Finally, cosmetic bags and toiletries go in last (for easy access).

83

Want to keep your collared shirts looking stiff? Roll up a belt and pop it inside the collar opening of the shirt. This will also save you a little bit of space.

84

Stop buying brand-new small travel containers of toothpaste, mouthwash, hand sanitizer, and so on, for each trip. Just refill old travel containers with the big bottles at home.

85

Always make sure to go for a test walk once you've packed for a backpacking trip. That way you can repack to make it lighter, or alter it to make it more comfortable before you leave. The last thing you want to do is test it when you get off the plane.

86

Unless you're going to the Antarctic, you can usually save a lot of space in your suitcase by wearing multiple layers, as opposed to packing a big puffy jacket or thick wool sweater.

87

Only need a little bit of makeup, lotion, sunscreen, and so on, for the day? Instead of bringing entire bottles, save room in your bag by putting these skin-care products in old contact lens cases.

88

Bought a new pair of shoes for your trip? Pack some extra thick socks to go with them. Wearing thick socks for the first couple of days can help wear in the shoes and prevent blisters.

89

You can keep your necklaces free from tangling in your suitcase by threading them through a straw and closing the clasp.

90

If you're the kind of person who brings a ton of hair ties, try looping them through a carabiner. It will keep them organized and all in one place while traveling.

91

Take certain medications on a regular basis? Pack them in smaller bunches in separate suitcases and carry-on bags. If one gets lost, you'll still have a week or so worth of your medication.

92

Light sleeper? Make sure to pack a pair of earplugs or noise-canceling headphones for your flight or if you're staying downtown in a busy city.

93

CONCERNED THAT THE ZIPPERS ON YOUR SUITCASE MIGHT OPEN? USE ZIP TIES TO FASTEN TOGETHER THE TWO ZIPPERS. THIS WILL MAKE IT IMPOSSIBLE FOR YOUR SUITCASE TO OPEN ACCIDENTALLY. (AND IF SECURITY DOES SEARCH YOUR BAG AND CUT THE TIES, YOU'RE ONLY OUT A FEW CENTS ON THE DOLLAR.)

94

Worried about your flight being late or delayed? Statistically, the four airlines with the best on-time arrival records are Delta, United, Alaska, and Hawaiian.

95

Keep the shape of your bras intact by nesting your socks inside the cups.

96

Scared of your liquid products leaking in your suitcase? Buy a pack of balloons at the dollar store and wrap them around the tops of the bottles. They'll be airtight and also waterproof.

97

Planning on bringing home a lot of stuff? Buy a smaller suitcase for your clothes and put it inside a bigger one.

98

Pack a small bottle of prescription medication. As long as it has your name on it, it can be used as a form of identification at airports, just in case you lose yours.

99

Packing some bottles that could potentially leak? Get some reassurance by wrapping some plastic wrap under the caps for backup.

Not Sure How Much You Can Carry in Your Carry-On? Use This Carry-On Luggage Size Chart

100 **Air China:** 22″ × 16″ × 8″ (max: Economy, 11 pounds/ Business, 2 pieces of luggage, 17 pounds each)

101 **American Airlines:** 22″ × 14″ × 9″ (max: undisclosed)

102 **Delta Air Lines:** 22″ × 14″ × 9″ (max: 15 pounds when flying out of Singapore Changi Airport, 22 pounds when flying out of Beijing Capital Airport and Shanghai Pudong Airport)

103 **EasyJet:** 22″ × 17.7″ × 9.8″ (max: undisclosed)

104 **Emirates:** 22″ × 15″ × 8″ (max: 15 pounds)

105 **Quantas:** 22″ × 14.2″ × 9″ (max: 15 pounds)

106 **Ryanair:** 21.7″ × 15.7″ × 7.9″ (max: 22 pounds)

107 **Southwest Airlines:** 24″ × 16″ × 10″ (max: 15.4 pounds)

108 **Turkish Airlines:** 21.7″ × 15.7″ × 9″ (max: 17.6 pounds)

109 **United Airlines:** 22″ × 14″ × 9″ (max: undisclosed)

110

Buy yourself a "travel towel." They're lightweight, dry more quickly, and fold up to half the size of a normal towel.

111

Always make sure to pack your pajamas and bedtime stuff last. When you get to your destination, you won't have to dig through the contents of your entire suitcase to get ready for sleep.

Chapter 3

BEFORE
YOU LEAVE

112

Always make sure to email yourself a photo or scan of your passport. Although this isn't good enough to get you on a plane, it can make the process much smoother if you ever lose or get your passport stolen.

113

Take a quick photo of yourself with your luggage before leaving for the airport. In the unfortunate event that your luggage gets lost, the photo helps the airline track it down and proves that you own it.

114

It's always a good idea to bring copies of important documents (such as a passport, travel insurance, health card, and so on). If somehow you lose everything, however, it's always a bonus if you've also stored all that stuff in the cloud.

115

Want to deter burglars from making your house a target? Connect certain lights in your house to timers to make them go on and off, and it will look like you're home.

116

Divide your money into roughly three equal amounts and place in three separate spots: one-third in your wallet, one-third in your suitcase, one-third in a handbag/man bag. If you get mugged or lose one of these items, you'll still have some money.

117

Want to ensure that you don't forget your passport? Put it in your shoe so you can't leave without stepping on it.

118

Be aware of the type of electrical outlets used in the country you are visiting. Now is the time to check and buy the appropriate power adapter. The last thing you want to be doing when you get to your destination is scouring stores for one.

119

Who said you need to own a business to have a business card? Print out some personal cards with your name, phone number, email, *Twitter*, *Facebook*, *Instagram*, and so on, and give them out to the friends you meet on your trip.

120

Always let your bank know you'll be traveling. Oftentimes, when banks see unusual transactions happening abroad, they'll block your card.

121

Different countries may have arbitrary preboarding requirements, like gate closure timings. Make sure you find out what these are ahead of your trip.

122

Pay your bills before you leave. It's probably the last thing you want to be doing, but companies still charge you interest and late charges if you're on vacation.

123

Some credit cards and bank accounts give you free airport lounge access. Check yours out before leaving, because you might have access to these spots and not even know it.

124

IF YOU'RE TRAVELING TO A DIFFERENT COUNTRY, TAKE A SECOND TO RESEARCH HOW THE PEOPLE THERE GREET ONE ANOTHER. SOME CULTURES REQUIRE A FIRM HANDSHAKE; SOME REQUIRE A LOOSER HANDSHAKE; SOME REQUIRE A BOW; SOME REQUIRE EYE CONTACT; SOME GREET THE OLDEST IN THE GROUP FIRST; AND SOME THINK IT'S INAPPROPRIATE TO SHAKE THE HAND OF A WOMAN.

125

Figure out your airport's Wi-Fi password in advance. You don't want to spend all your time hunting around for it once you are there. Google has a page of wireless passwords from airports and lounges around the world. Also check out your destination airport's password for the way home too.

126

Always take a picture or screenshot of your itinerary and hotel information before you go on a work trip. This will save you from being late or a "no-show" if you can't get access to the Internet or data.

127

Traveling with expensive items like a laptop, camera, and so on? Write down all of their serial numbers before you leave. If they're stolen, having this information will make it so much easier to get them back from the police.

128

Not sure of what weather to expect at a location? Check out the location tag for that spot on *Instagram*. This will give you an idea of what to wear and pack for your trip.

129

Make sure you adjust your home's thermostat up/down before you leave on your trip to save money—but don't turn it off completely. Your house needs air circulation to control humidity and mold.

130

Before going on vacation, place a coin on a mug of ice in your freezer. On return, if the coin is in the ice, it means your freezer stopped working at one point, and your food has gone bad.

131

Bringing a bunch of souvenirs back for friends and family? Make a list of those you need to buy for before you leave. This way you won't have to think on the spot and run the risk of forgetting someone.

132

Going on a long trip? Do something weird or abnormal when locking your front door so you can easily remember that you did it.

133

Going away for longer than a week and don't want your mail to pile up in your mailbox? Contact your local post office, tell them the dates you'll be away, and they'll hold your mail and then deliver it when you get back.

134

The ASRS (Aviation Safety Reporting System) is a reporting system designed by NASA that allows flight crews to confidentially report near-miss or close-call incidents during flights without fear of losing their jobs. The entire database is available to the public at https://asrs.arc.nasa.gov/search/database.html. You can use the ASRS to check out the airline you're using from inside the organization.

135

Take a picture of a map of your destination on your phone before leaving. Most cameras are high enough resolution that you can zoom in to any spot clearly.

136

Save all those small free sample packs of lotion, soap, shampoo, and so on in the weeks leading up to your trip. These are perfect for traveling because they take up very little space.

137

You can get notified by the US Embassy when there's a natural disaster, civil unrest, or emergency by enrolling your trip on *STEP* (Smart Traveler Enrollment Program) at https://step.state.gov.

138

Before you leave, pour some baking soda and vinegar down your drains. This will help keep your drains and pipes fresh while you're away.

139

Looking for a camera to document your travels? Go to *Flickr* (www.flickr.com/cameras), browse photos by the camera that was used to shoot them, and find the model that matches your needs.

140

TRAVELING WITH SOME
BIRTHDAY OR HOLIDAY GIFTS
FOR PEOPLE? OFTENTIMES,
IT CAN BE CHEAPER TO
SHIP THESE ITEMS TO THE
DESTINATION INSTEAD.
MOST AIRLINES CHARGE $35
FOR ADDITIONAL BAGS; IF
IT'S HEAVY, IT CAN COST
YOU AN EXTRA $50.

141

One of the best things you can do before you leave for the airport is to hit the gym! Exercising helps reduce the stress of flying. It will also help you get to sleep, and you won't fidget as much when you have to stay virtually still for hours on end.

142

Always change your sheets, and do laundry and a quick cleaning before you leave. There's nothing worse than coming home from a vacation and having to do housework. Your future self will thank you!

143

Get a few extra passport photos to take with you on your trip. If something happens, the last thing you want to be doing is roaming around a foreign town looking for someone to take a photo for you.

Before You Leave, Make Sure These Things Are in Your Carry-On Bag

144 Passport/ID

145 Headphones

146 Socks

147 Deodorant

148 Eye mask

149 Reusable water bottle

150 Book(s)

151 Neck pillow

152 Snacks

153 Extra outfit

154

Have an early flight out? Put on your deodorant the night before. Not only is it one less thing you have to do before your flight; it's also been proven to be more effective than morning applications at stopping that nervous underarm sweat.

155

Looking to spice up your foreign vocabulary before you travel? You can learn Spanish, French, Italian, German, and Portuguese for free on *Duolingo*.

156

Going somewhere warm? Eat a lot of tomatoes the week before you leave. They have been known to prevent sunburn and are an effective natural defense against sun damage.

157

To get rid of your flying anxiety, try this breathing exercise: Exhale completely, inhale for four seconds, hold your breath for seven seconds, and then exhale for eight seconds.

158

Before leaving, make yourself a meal or two, and put them in the freezer. You'll thank yourself later when you get home and are too tired to cook.

159

If you're planning on going away for a significant amount of time, try to book a quick health checkup with your doctor before you go. It's much better to find out something before you leave than when you're abroad.

160

When painting your nails before a trip, pick a lighter color. Lighter nail polish shades don't show chips or cracks nearly as badly as darker shades do.

161

Never underestimate the power of a fanny pack. They may not be the most fashion-forward choice, but these things can save you several headaches throughout the day— and they're almost impossible to steal!

Chapter 4

AIR TRAVEL

162

Having a tough time saying goodbye to loved ones at the airport? You can request an escort pass to go through security and all the way to the gate with them until they board the plane.

163

Did you know you can bring alcohol onto an airplane? As long as it's in bottles of 3.4 ounces or smaller, it is acceptable to carry it onboard.

164

Hate emptying out your pockets every time you go through a security line? Put it all in your jacket pockets, then just throw your jacket in a bin.

165

Airport security scanners have trouble scanning glittery sweaters or any clothing with something shiny on it. So, if you're wearing something of this nature, expect to be searched and patted down.

166

If you decide to volunteer to give up your seat on an overbooked flight, don't just take the offer. Tell the gate agent to "toss in another $200 (or more/less depending on your best judgment), and I'll go for it." They'll almost always say okay, because a willing volunteer is worth it.

167

Always pack an extra pillow case in your carry-on. That way if you ever have a long flight delay or get stuck somewhere, you always have the option to stuff it with clothes for a makeshift pillow.

168

When you are handed a luggage claim ticket, immediately take a picture of it with your phone. If it becomes lost, you can still claim your property without a hassle.

169

Suitcase a little too full? Put on a few extra layers and take them off when you get on the plane.

170

Hate waiting in customs or security lines? If you're a frequent flyer, it might be worth it to apply for Global Entry. This US Customs and Border Protection program requires an interview and costs $100 for a five-year membership, but it will let you skip every single TSA and customs line on your journey.

171

Feel like you're going to vomit on the plane? Eating a mint or chewing some minty gum may help you control the urge to vomit.

172

Want to make friends while traveling? Bring a power strip to the airport. You'll be a hero and meet a ton of new people.

173

Speed up airport security lines for you and everyone else by knowing how many bins you'll need: one per backpack/briefcase, one specifically for each laptop, one for your shoes, and one for all other personal items (belt, wallet, cell phone, watch).

174

FORGET TO BRING A NECK
PILLOW? YOU CAN MAKE ONE
BY ROLLING UP AN AIRLINE
BLANKET AND WEARING
IT LIKE A SCARF. IT'S
OBVIOUSLY NOT AS COMFY,
BUT IT WILL AT LEAST KEEP
YOUR HEAD IN ONE PLACE
WHILE YOU TAKE A NAP.

175

Want to find the best spot to eat at an airport? Look for where the flight attendants and flight crews are eating. Chances are they've been there many times and know where the best spots are.

176

Flight get canceled? Instead of rushing the ticket agent with the rest of the travelers, call the airline's 1-800 number. They can do the exact same stuff as the agent can, and you'll beat 90 percent of the line by doing so.

177

Always make sure to pack a pen in your carry-on before you leave for your flight. This will make your life so much easier when it comes to filling in forms.

178

When going through security lines, always go to the one that's farthest to the left. Due to the fact that most people are right-handed, they tend to favor going to lines on the right.

179

Before takeoff, download a few of your favorite podcasts while you have Wi-Fi. Listening to them is a great way to pass the time on those long flights, and you won't be able to access them unless you're planning on paying for the onboard Internet.

180

Trying to kill time on a long flight? Download a Game Boy emulator on your phone and replay some childhood games like *Pokémon*. The flight will "fly" by.

181

Hate traveling with all those loose cords? Bring an extra glasses case and store them in there for easy access and to keep them tangle-free.

182

Never be afraid of asking for an upgrade on your airplane. Oftentimes business or first class isn't full and some airlines will upgrade you for free. The worst thing that can happen is they say no.

183

If you miss your departing flight, you're marked by the airline as a "no-show," which means the return part of your ticket is considered forfeit.

184

Buy a portable phone charger. You'll be using your phone on your flight and while waiting for your flight, and you don't want to arrive at your destination with no power. A portable charger is inexpensive, easy to pack, and will prevent so many headaches!

185

Always make sure to bring an empty water bottle with you while flying. Airports are stricter about liquids (even if it's only water), but if you bring an empty bottle, you'll be able to fill it once you get through security.

186

If you are denied boarding or your flight is canceled, know that the check-in counter or boarding gate legally has to tell you your rights. This can be especially useful when it comes to claiming compensation assistance.

187

Shoes stink from traveling all day? Throw them in your freezer when you get to your hotel. It will kill the bacteria and get rid of the stink.

188

Always take a screenshot of your mobile boarding pass before you leave for the airport. You don't want to have to rely on an Internet connection to be able to get on your plane.

189

Want to add some comfort and lumbar support to your seat? Roll up a blanket or jacket, and place it on the lower seat back. This will help support your back much better than the normal C-shaped airplane seat.

190

No in-flight entertainment? A crushed-up soda can or a zip-top bag make for perfect TV stands for watching something on your phone.

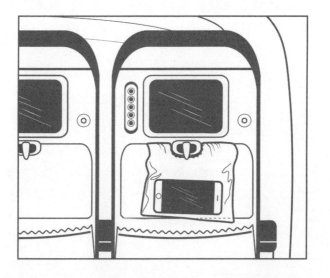

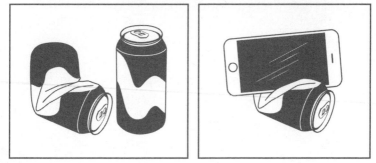

191

Traveling to Australia or New Zealand? Declare your shoes as "used outdoor equipment." The "declare" line is always way shorter than the normal TSA line.

192

Looking for a way to stop your feet from swelling up while in the air? Buy some compression socks.

193

Stop worrying about getting that dreaded middle seat; book your seat online in advance to get your choice of seats. Most airlines let you book online up to twenty-four hours before your flight. So don't leave it to the last minute!

194

There's a reason airline food never tastes that good. Our sense of smell and taste decreases by 20 to 50 percent in the extremely dry air caused by the low air pressure and humidity of an airplane flying at a cruising altitude of 30,000 to 35,000 feet. One way to combat this is to bring your own packet of salt.

195

Throw a stick of lip balm and a small tube of moisturizer in your carry-on. The air in planes is notorious for being super dry. Just make sure your bottle of moisturizer is small enough to clear through security.

196

Traveling as a couple? Try booking the window and aisle seat of a row. If the flight isn't full you'll likely have the full row to yourselves, and if someone books it, they'll most likely switch with you because who the heck wants to sit in the middle seat?

Know Your Flight Attendant Slang

 Blue juice: The water inside the toilet.

Bottle-to-throttle: The amount of time a pilot must abstain from consuming alcohol before flying.

Crotch watch: The time dedicated to making sure people have their seatbelt fastened properly.

Deadhead: A member of the crew who is on the flight to hitch a ride somewhere.

Gate lice: People who are clustered around the front of the airplane.

George: A nickname for the airplane's autopilot.

Mini me: The small garbage bag used to pick up trash from passengers.

Slinging hash: Meal service time.

Steerage: The section of the flight with the cheapest seats.

 Two-for-one special: When the plane bounces off the ground during landing.

207

Hate that ear-popping sound you get when taking off/landing? Buy some altitude ear plugs. They're specially designed to reduce the pressure in your ears and only cost about $8 online.

208

Want to feel like a VIP at the airport? Most of those executive lounges offer day passes. This can be of value if you ever have a long layover.

209

Looking for a way to get through airport security faster? Get in line with all the business travelers. They are usually in a rush, travel light, and know the drill.

210

Alternatively, the slowest people to get behind in an airport security line are families, especially ones with multiple kids. Avoid these lines and your life will be much easier.

211

Want to spot your bag in no time at baggage claim? Tie a piece of brightly colored ribbon to it.

212

If you're traveling in Europe and your flight is delayed three or more hours, be aware that you are entitled to certain compensation, which can be anything from free meals right up to 600 euros, depending on the situation. Make sure to always check your airline's policy about compensation for flight delays.

213

Most airlines have an app that lets you check in and print your boarding pass before you arrive at the airport. This way, you can skip the check-in line and go straight to security, potentially cutting your wait time in half.

214

If Uber and Lyft prices are surging at the airport, try taking the shuttle bus one stop away from the airport. This can reduce the cost by over 60 percent.

215

Want more attentive service from flight attendants? Sit in the rear of the plane. Flight attendants often discourage extras for passengers in the front of the plane, because they have to walk by all the other passengers to get to the front, creating more demand. Sit in the back, however, and no one else will see you get that extra mini bottle of tequila.

216

Never exchange your cash at airports. Those currency conversions stands are known for having the worst exchange rates.

217

Want to promote good circulation in your feet? Buy an airplane foot rest. They sling over your tray table so you can kick up your feet and relax. You can grab one online for about $20.

218

Start to feel yourself losing your voice during a flight? Drink some water immediately. It's pretty common for people to lose their voices due to the lack of moisture inside airplanes, so make sure you stay hydrated (not with coffee or soda but with water).

Chapter 5

ROAD TRIPPING AND OTHER TRANSPORTATION

219

Exit numbers on highways in most US states correlate with the miles of the highway. For example, Exit 75 is about 75 miles down the highway. This can be useful to keep track of how many miles you have to travel until your exit.

220

If you ever get trapped underwater in your car, use your car seat headrest to break the window.

221

Whatever amount of time a road trip took you in the past, be sure to add about 5 to 10 percent more time the next time. Traffic, especially in cities, is constantly getting worse, especially during rush hour. Think of it like inflation for driving times.

222

Stuff a zip-top plastic bag with some napkins and plastic utensils and stash it in your car. It's guaranteed to come in handy at some point during a road trip.

223

Fighting sleep while on a long drive? Find the nearest Walmart. They don't have time limits on parking in their parking lots, so you're legally allowed to park your car, truck, or RV there overnight.

224

Making a playlist for your road trip? Add some songs by the people who produced your favorite artists. The producer usually has a big part in how the final song sounds, plus these songs will be unique to your trip—forever—and will "take you back" every time they come on.

225

Want to be the first to get a cab at the airport?
Don't follow the crowd to the taxis outside of
Arrivals; instead, head to Departures, and you'll find
plenty of empty ones that just dropped off people.

226

Avoid overpaying for taxis in other countries
by opening your phone's GPS and entering
the coordinates for the destination yourself.

227

If you're too young to rent a car, rent a
U-Haul. You only need to be eighteen years
old to rent one, and they have some smaller
van options that are better on gas.

228

Parking at the airport or other multistory lot?
Take a picture of your section/row so you don't
spend hours walking around trying to find it.

229

Staying hydrated is key for any road trip. The best places to fill your water jug for free are national parks, gas stations, cafés, or restaurants.

230

Getting drowsy during a long drive? Listen to standup comedy. This will make the time go by more quickly—and it's almost impossible to fall asleep while you're laughing.

231

When driving over 40 mph, it is more economical to have the windows up and the AC on. When driving under 40 mph, the opposite is true.

232

Taking a Greyhound bus across the country? Note that your ticket is good for a whole year, so you can stop off at transfer points, explore/experience the area, and then hop back on another bus.

233

Traffic lights out or flashing red? This means you're legally obligated to treat it like a stop sign, even if there are no other cars around.

234

Want to stay eco-friendly while traveling? Select "Green Mode" when requesting a Lyft. This will guarantee that the car that is coming to pick you up is either a hybrid or electric car for the same price as a gasoline-powered one.

235

Feel yourself falling asleep on those early morning drives? Order a cup of ice with your morning coffee and chew on the cubes while driving. This works better than the coffee at keeping you awake.

236

IN MOST CITIES, THE
HIGHER THE SPEED LIMIT,
THE LONGER THE YELLOW
LIGHT WILL BE. BE CAREFUL
IF YOU START SLOWING
DOWN TOO EARLY AT A LONG
YELLOW LIGHT; YOU MIGHT
GET HIT FROM BEHIND.

237

Due to the pressure and wear and tear on your tires, you're often going slower than what your car's speedometer indicates. In some cars, this can vary as much as 3.1 mph.

238

As much as you may think speeding will get you there faster, it's actually not the case in high-traffic areas. If you go the exact speed limit, you'll hit more consecutive green lights in areas with lots of stoplights.

239

When visiting national parks, keep in mind that most of the parks offer shuttle buses from nearby parking lots. This will help you avoid crowds, and you may also get discounts on some state park entrance fees.

240

If you ever get lost while on the road, don't stop at a gas station for directions; instead, stop at a pizza place. Because of their deliveries, they know where everything is!

241

You can find out where you board a train by looking for the dirty spots on the yellow caution paint—this is usually where all the foot traffic is.

242

Before leaving on a road trip, stash a gallon jug of water somewhere in your car. It takes up minimal space and may just help you stay hydrated until you get to the nearest gas station.

243

Before paying for transportation in other countries (such as for train tickets, domestic flights, and so on), check the website in the country's native language. Some countries in South America and Asia offer cheaper fares on these websites.

244

Going on a road trip to somewhere colder? Make sure to check your tire pressure; for every 10-degree drop in air temperature, tire pressure decreases by 1 pound per square inch. It can make a big difference as you move from temperatures in the 80s to the 30s.

245

When renting a car, one of the first things you should do is hit the alarm button to get familiar with that sound.

246

Bear in mind that there are specific blow-up mattresses (available for sale online) that are designed to turn the back seat of your car into a bed.

247

Going just 5 mph over the 25 mph speed limit in a residential neighborhood or school district bumps up the pedestrian fatality rate by 75 percent. That's why the 25 mph speed limit was chosen.

248

Not sure where the entrance to an airport or hotel is? Look for where the handicapped parking is. These are always located as close as possible to the main entrance.

249

If the taxi driver asks if you're "from around here," lie and say yes. Sometimes they travel farther (driving up the price) for tourists.

250

Car battery doesn't want to turn over on a cold morning? Don't keep trying to crank the key. Instead, turn on the headlights for about thirty seconds and try again. This can work like a charm.

251

Want to remember where you parked your car? Use the Google Maps app to track where you park. Just tap your current location when you park and "star" the location.

252

Whenever you fill up your tires with air, make sure to check your spare tire too. There's no point in carrying around a spare one if you can't use it.

253

YOU CAN INCREASE YOUR FUEL EFFICIENCY BY 10 PERCENT BY REPLACING AN OLD AIR FILTER. YOU CAN INCREASE IT BY 25 PERCENT BY REMOVING YOUR ROOFTOP CARGO CARRIER. AND FOR EVERY 100 POUNDS OF WEIGHT YOU REMOVE, YOU'LL INCREASE FUEL EFFICIENCY BY 1 PERCENT.

254

Whenever you see an animal crossing the road, always assume that there will be others following it. Most wildlife like to travel in packs while following each other, so make sure to drive with caution.

255

Worried about which side of the road your exit will be on? If an exit number is on the top right side of the sign, the exit will be on the right side of the road. If the exit number is on the top left side of the sign, the exit will be on the left side of the road.

256

If someone flashes their high beams, it means there is a police officer ahead. If they flick their lights on and off, it means your headlights are off.

257

The SitOrSquat app will show you the cleanest public bathrooms when you're on the road.

258

The Along the Way app will look for cool attractions you can see along the way of any road trip.

259

At a gas pump that has one of those video screens blaring annoying ads while you pump? Press the secret mute button on the right side of the screen, usually located one button down.

260

The best way to get rid of car sickness during long road trips is to tilt your head sideways.

261

Never put your feet up on a car's dashboard. Airbags can go off like small bombs and they can easily break both of your legs.

262

If you're planning a road trip during the winter, apply some cooking spray to the cracks of the doors before you leave. This will prevent your doors from freezing shut.

263

You can make sure your locks will never freeze up by spraying them with a little WD-40.

264

If normal car rental services are sold out or don't have what you need, try out *Turo*. It's a car-sharing marketplace that's like the *Airbnb* for cars. People post their vehicles for rent, usually at cheaper rates than car rental companies.

265

Getting a cab in Las Vegas? Kindly remind the cab driver not to take the highway. Taking the highway from the airport to the Strip nearly doubles the mileage and the price.

266

Having a hard time staying in your lane because of the glare from oncoming car lights? The best way to make sure you're staying in your lane is to follow the solid white line on the edge of the roadway, where the shoulder begins. This will be much less distracting to follow.

267

HAVE A LONG DRIVE AHEAD?
ALWAYS MAKE SURE TO
OCCASIONALLY TURN DOWN
THE MUSIC AND LISTEN TO
YOUR CAR FOR A COUPLE
MINUTES. BY CATCHING A
RATTLING ENGINE, BROKEN
MUFFLER, OR SOMETHING
SIMILAR EARLY ON, YOU CAN
SAVE YOURSELF FROM BEING
IN A MUCH WORSE SITUATION
DOWN THE ROAD. THIS
PREVENTIVE MEASURE COULD
SAVE YOUR ENTIRE TRIP.

268

Lock your keys in your car? Don't call a locksmith—just order the AAA basic membership package, and they'll send a locksmith as part of their roadside service. AAA membership costs $66 (versus $100 for a locksmith). Plus, if it ever happens again within the year, you're covered.

269

Stuck in traffic on the highway? Pay attention to the lanes that semitrucks are merging into and follow them. They usually use a CB radio or smartphone to communicate which lanes are blocked or shut down from an accident.

270

The Fibonacci Sequence can help you convert between miles and kilometers. All you have to do is add the sum of the two previous ones to find the next number in the series. For example, 5 mi = 8 km, 8 mi = 13 km, 13 mi = 21 km, and so on.

271

If you're on the road and have to use the bathroom, find the nearest hotel. Their bathrooms are much cleaner than gas station ones.

272

No TV in your car to entertain passengers? Use a visor mount to hang a tablet off your car's sun visor for some onboard entertainment.

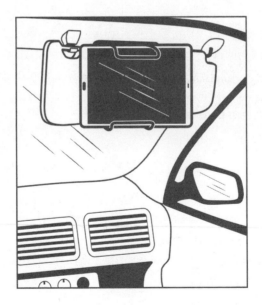

273

Feeling seasick on a boat/cruise? Try eating some ginger. It's an age-old natural remedy for treating nausea and motion sickness. Some cruise ships keep a secret stash to give out to guests.

274

Before heading out on a road trip, always stop by a bank or change machine to grab a few rolls of quarters. They're perfect for paying the tolls or feeding the parking meters that you'll surely run into.

275

When using a taxi, always get a receipt from the driver. If you accidentally leave something behind, you have the company name, contact number, and taxi number you left it in.

How to Jump-Start a Car

(WRITE THIS DOWN OR TAKE A PICTURE
OF THIS PAGE FOR REFERENCE)

276 Turn off both cars.

277 Clamp RED jumper cable end on dead car's positive battery terminal (+).

278 Clamp the other RED jumper cable on the working car's positive battery terminal (+).

279 Clamp BLACK end on the working car's negative battery terminal (-).

280 Clamp the other BLACK end on an unpainted metal surface on dead car.

281 Start the working car.

282 Start your dead car.

283 Remove clamps in reverse order that you put them on.

284 Drive for at least fifteen minutes to charge your car.

285

You can use toothpaste to clear up your hazy car headlights. Put a blob of toothpaste on a rag or cloth, and scrub the headlight. Works like magic.

286

Turn your steering wheel 180 degrees before parking in the sun. This way, you won't burn your hands when you start driving.

287

Keep blankets, water, nonperishable snacks, and a small toolkit in your vehicle in case you have any car troubles on the road.

288

Bring an extra battery for your car's key fob. You don't want to get locked out of your car while on your road trip.

289

CAR GET STUCK IN THE MUD OR SNOW? YOU CAN GET SOME TRACTION BY THROWING A FLOOR MAT UPSIDE DOWN UNDER THE BACK TIRES (FOR REAR WHEEL DRIVE) OR THE FRONT TIRES (FOR FRONT WHEEL DRIVE).

290

Looking to hit the spa on your cruise?
Try booking it on a port day; there will
be way less people there. Cruises often
do special deals because of this.

291

Enter your route in the GasBuddy app,
and it will show you the cheapest gas
prices in real time along the way.

292

Need a little freshening up on a long drive?
Most truck stops will let you use their facilities,
including the showers, for a small fee.

293

You can make a DIY garbage can for
your car by simply lining a plastic cereal
container with a small trash bag.

Chapter 6

TRAVELING
WITH KIDS
AND PETS

294

Heading out to a safari, zoo, marine land, or somewhere with animals? Find out beforehand what color clothing the employees wear—and wear the same color. The animals will come right up to you instead of backing away.

295

Family trip to the beach? Throw a hand brush in the car before you go. You'll easily be able to get all the sand off your feet before getting in the car. You can also use an ice scraper left over from the winter.

296

Looking for a pet-friendly hotel? La Quinta and Red Roof Inn are the most popular hotel chains for pets around. If you can't find one of those nearby, peruse the local tourism boards for suggestions.

297

Drinking a warm cup of water right after takeoff and about forty-five minutes before landing can really help mitigate any ear pain or discomfort that younger children experience due to the sudden change in air pressure.

298

Before taking your pet to a new country, make sure you research the embassy requirements for bringing animals into the country. Some countries require a quarantine period, along with shots for rabies, *Bordetella* (kennel cough), and parvo.

299

You can get a free baby bassinet on a plane. Some airlines have them onboard, and some have to be ordered beforehand, so make sure to contact the airline before your flight.

300

DRIVING CROSS-COUNTRY WITH YOUR DOG? YOU SHOULD BE AWARE THAT SOME STATE LAWS (IN NEW JERSEY, RHODE ISLAND, AND MORE) REQUIRE THAT YOUR DOG WEAR A SEAT BELT OR BE KEPT IN A CRATE. SIMPLY HAVING YOUR DOG SITTING IN THE BACK SEAT OF YOUR CAR CAN RESULT IN A FINE OF UP TO $1,000.

301

Do your kid's ears hurt during plane flights? Take two cups and put paper towels wet (not dripping) with hot water inside the cups, then have your child hold the cups over their ears like headphones. This will give them almost instant relief from the pain.

302

If your dog is prone to anxiety, one of the best things you can do is put a T-shirt or small blanket you've recently used inside his crate.

303

When flying with a child on your lap, *do not* fasten the seat belt around both of you. If the plane suddenly stops or thrusts forward, it can actually injure your child much worse than if she had fallen out of your arms. Some airlines actually offer an adaptable seat belt that loops inside yours and goes around your child.

304

Let your kids pick out a bright and colorful luggage tag. When it's time to wait for your luggage, they'll stay close and attentive because searching for their luggage becomes a fun "eye spy" game.

305

Taking your pet on a road trip? To prevent scratches in your car seats buy a good securely fitting seat cover for the spot your pet will be. This will also help prevent the infamous "furry" car seat.

306

Make sure to throw a stain remover pen (such as the Tide-to-Go pen) in your bag before heading out for the day. Stains are like magnets to kids on vacation; it's almost guaranteed you'll use it!

307

Dining in your hotel room and need a makeshift table for the kids to eat at? Cover the ironing board in an extra sheet to make an impromptu dining table.

308

Before taking your kid to a busy amusement park, write your contact info on their wrists and cover it with a liquid bandage. If they get lost, they will have your contact number, and the liquid bandage will stop it from rubbing off.

309

A lollipop alleviates that taking off/landing ear popping and pain in kids over three years old. Plus, it's guaranteed to keep them entertained for a bit.

310 Avoid going to Disneyland on the weekends. During this time, the locals bring their kids on their days off, so it tends to get crowded.

311 Anyone buying a 3-Day Disney Theme Park Ticket with Park Hopper option gets to enter Disneyland Park one hour early on Tuesday, Thursday, or Saturday. These are the days you should visit California Adventure first because there are so many crowds at the main park.

312 There is a "Magic Hour" where guests staying at Disney resorts can get into the park an hour earlier than the general admission. The Disneyland Park days are Tuesdays, Thursdays, and Saturdays; and the California Adventure Park days are Mondays, Wednesdays, Fridays, and Sundays.

313 You can request a wake-up call from a Disney character at Disney-owned hotels by calling the front desk. Imagine your kids' surprise at being woken up by Mickey or Minnie in the morning.

314 Wherever you stay in Anaheim, there is an ART (Anaheim Resort Transportation) shuttle that picks up guests who are staying at hotels near the park. This is a great option for getting to the park if you can't walk there.

315 If your kids hate waiting in lines, you can purchase a FastPass for some of the more popular attractions.

316 Reservations for restaurants at Disney can be made sixty days in advance. Make sure you take advantage of these booking times to avoid eating fair food your entire day.

317 If you're staying at a Disneyland hotel, you don't have to carry around your purchases all day. You can have them sent directly back to your hotel room. This perk is ideal if you want to buy your children stuffed animals or souvenirs that can easily be lost at the park.

318 Make sure you save room for the Candy Palace. The candy apples there are legendary, and they have a new flavor created each month, such as triple chocolate or peanut clusters.

319 If your goal is to take a photo with the Disney princesses, then head over to Fantasy Faire. Make sure that you plan this part of your day for early in the morning, when the lines are the shortest.

320

If you're traveling with your family, throw everyone's sleepwear and toothbrushes in one easy-to-reach bag. That way, when you get to your destination, you won't have to fumble through a bunch of suitcases to get ready for bed on the first night.

321

Going out for the day with the kids? Grab half a roll of toilet paper or some tissues and put them in your backpack. You'll most likely use them at some point during the day.

322

Avoid the inevitable "Are we there yet?" question by attaching a laminated travel map to the back of the front seat and having your kids trace the route by crossing off landmarks.

323

Make sure to keep a copy of your pet's veterinary health certificate while traveling. Many hotels, travel operators, pet care centers, and airlines won't accept your pet without this.

324

Vacationing in a warm place with your pup? Try giving him an ice cube/ice chips instead of water. This will give him both a cold drink as it melts and a fun toy to play with!

325

Pack a lint roller—it picks up more than lint. Use it to collect glitter, sprinkles, cereal, and many other small things that kids spill all over the place.

326

Want to cut down on the amount of toiletries you have to bring? Just bring baby shampoo and baby wash. They both work just as well on adults.

327

Road tripping with the kids? Fill some leftover plastic Easter eggs with their favorite snacks and then hand them out when hunger sets in. The snacks will take care of the hunger, and the eggs will entertain your kids for at least a little while.

328

Always make sure to pack a spare set of clothes for your kids in your carry-on. You'll be glad you did when a messy moment arises.

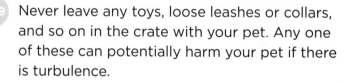

Five Tips for Flying with Your Pet

329 Never leave any toys, loose leashes or collars, and so on in the crate with your pet. Any one of these can potentially harm your pet if there is turbulence.

330 Finding it hard to get your pet inside the crate? Stop treating it like a prison. Use a happy voice and make it an exciting experience.

331 Avoid feeding your pet for a few hours before flying. This way, they won't have a full bladder and stomach for the whole flight.

332 Give them plenty of exercise prior to takeoff.

333 Crate your pet before you get to the airport. It will be a lot easier to do so in an environment that is calmer than a busy airport.

334

Scared of getting separated from your kids in a crowded area? Have them download Life360 to their phone. As long as the designated phone is on, this app tracks their location in real time.

335

Always ask airport security where the family-friendly TSA lane is. Most airports have kid-friendly lanes set up.

336

Kid got an injury but you forgot to pack an ice pack? Take some fast-food ketchup packets and stick them in the hotel fridge. They are perfectly kid-sized and pliable enough to form around most injury areas.

337

Try to plan feeding your dog after a long drive and not before. Dogs are actually more prone than humans to get motion sickness.

338

Flying with young kids? When the airline employee calls that first group of people who "need extra time to board," this includes you!

339

Want to keep your kids distracted in the airport? Play some "eye spy" bingo. Make a square bingo board and add things like an air traffic control tower, a bus, headphones, a rolling suitcase, a baby, a pilot, a cell phone, someone on a laptop, a hamburger, a policeman, a plane, someone sleeping, a stroller, a flight attendant, a baggage cart, a metal detector, a clock, a newspaper, a drink cart, and anything else you'd find on an airplane or in an airport terminal.

340

Planning on taking your new pet abroad? Make sure they're at least eight weeks old. Airlines don't let pets aboard if they're younger than this.

341

Save your kids from getting hangry during a flight by bringing a few of their favorite snacks. Airlines usually don't have too many kid-friendly snack options.

342

Worried about people on the plane being annoyed by your baby/kids? Try handing out a "kid-proof" goodie bag. Include some ear plugs, eye mask, a few candies, and a note thanking them for their understanding.

343

WANT TO SAVE SOME MONEY
WHILE ON VACATION?
NEVER UNDERESTIMATE THE
VALUE OF THE "KIDS EAT
FREE" PROMOTIONS. MANY
PLACES AROUND THE WORLD
OFFER THIS AND USUALLY
HAVE THE DETAILS ABOUT
IT ON THEIR WEBSITES.

344

Most trains will let kids meet the conductor;
just ask someone who works there, and
they'll take you up to meet him/her.

345

Want your kid to behave during a flight? Buy them
a brand-new toy for the journey, and don't give it
to them until you're on the plane. You can even use
this as leverage for them to behave while boarding.

346

Before putting your pet in a crate, make sure to
attach their collar, leash, and harness. The last thing
you want to be doing is trying to attach these in a
busy airport after you've both had a long flight.

347

When going somewhere super busy with kids, like an amusement park, make sure to snap a quick photo of them at the beginning of the outing. This way, if they get lost, you can show people an up-to-date photo with exactly what they're wearing.

348

Always look up laws about traveling with pets in other states/countries, as they can differ from place to place.

Chapter 7

FOOD
AND
LODGING

349

If you want to book an all-inclusive vacation, it's better to book your hotel and then upgrade to an all-inclusive package when you check in. This way, you'll have the opportunity to look at what you're really getting. And in most cases, if you decide to upgrade, you'll get a much cheaper rate.

350

Looking for another way besides using extra salt to make your airplane food taste better? Pack your own spices in a sealed-off straw or small box, like a Tic Tac container. Then refill it with new spices from your destination for the trip home.

351

Park your car with the hotel valet? Go for breakfast first before getting your car. Usually everyone tries to get their car at around the hotel's checkout time. This can leave you waiting in excess of thirty to forty minutes.

352

SLEEPING IN A HOTEL ROOM CAN BE HARD ENOUGH WITHOUT THOSE LITTLE FLASHING LIGHTS ALL OVER THE ROOM (TELEPHONE, TV POWER, SMOKE DETECTORS, AND SO ON). MAKE SURE TO PACK A LITTLE ROLL OF ELECTRICAL TAPE SO YOU CAN BLOCK THEM OUT.

353

Use a soft-grip binder clip and an elastic band to make a DIY phone/GPS holder:

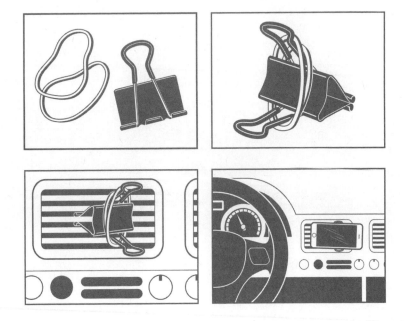

354

Scared that your drink will spill while you're in the car? Put some cling wrap over the top and poke a hole through it for a makeshift (adult) sip cup.

355

Some hotel minibars work on sensors, meaning you'll get charged just for taking an item out of its place. Always check your bill when leaving so you don't get charged for something you didn't have.

356

Always make sure to add your spouse's name to your hotel reservation. A lot of hotels aren't allowed to grant access or give additional keys to people who haven't been registered to the room, even if you have the same last name as them.

357

Want to save some cash on food? Use your hotel room's coffee maker to make foods like oatmeal, ramen, macaroni and cheese cups, and dry soup mixes.

358

Can't decide what to eat at a restaurant while traveling? You can never go wrong by ordering the chef's favorite dish.

359

The most common foods that cause food poisoning are chicken, shellfish, raw milk, eggs, sprouts, and raw flour or dough.

360

If the front desk of your hotel calls you to verify your credit card details, just go down and talk to them in person. It's a very common scam for people to call your room (which is easy to do) and pose as someone at the front desk.

361

Hit the wrong button on your hotel elevator? Press the same button again twice. This will undo the requested stop and avoid stopping at that floor.

362

If you are eating at a Japanese restaurant, don't rub your chopsticks together! This gesture is actually offensive to the restaurant because it suggests that you think their chopsticks are cheap and inferior.

363

BEFORE IRONING YOUR CLOTHES AT A HOTEL, SEND THE FIRST COUPLE OF PUFFS INTO A TOWEL. SOMETIMES HOTEL IRONS CAN GO UNUSED FOR MONTHS, AND THE STEAM HOLES CAN GET FILLED WITH SOME BROWN MINERAL DEPOSITS.

364

If you're traveling on a very small budget and need a place to crash, try looking up something called "dispersed camping," which is camping anywhere outside of a designated site. In these campsites, you're allowed to sleep in your car or pitch a tent for the night, free of charge. To find some really beautiful places, sift through reviews on apps like Campendium or iOverlander.

365

Looking for a last-minute dinner reservation? Use the OpenTable app. It shows you open reservations at nearby places with a simple one-click reservation. It's especially good if you're trying to book for a larger group.

366

If your hotel room doesn't have an iron, hang up your clothes in the bathroom and blast the shower at the hottest temperature possible. All the wrinkles will be gone within ten minutes.

367

Someone treating you to dinner but you don't know what price range to order in? Ask them what they recommend.

368

Hotel mirror keep fogging up? Rub a little soapy water on it before you shower or run the tap.

369

No laundry where you're staying? Pack some travel laundry detergent, like Tide Travel Sink Packets. They're like turning your sink into a washing machine.

370

Don't trust those hotel safes? You can bring your own portable safe, such as one from Master Lock, which locks onto things just like a bike lock.

371

Hotel door light go green but won't open? Try lifting up on the handle. The majority of guests push down to open the doors, which often grinds out these gears; but they work the same way if you pull up on them.

372

Instead of spending a fortune at the hotel bar, grab your favorite drinks at a nearby liquor store or gas station. Fill your sink with ice from the ice machine and use it as a cooler for your beverages.

373

Whenever you're out at a restaurant, make sure to wash your hands after reading the menu and ordering. Menus are generally the dirtiest thing you touch in a restaurant because everyone has touched them, and they very seldom get washed down.

Ten Countries Where Tipping Is Not Customary

374 Australia

375 Belgium

376 Brazil

377 China

378 Denmark

379 Estonia

380 Japan

381 New Zealand

382 South Korea

383 Switzerland

384

Forget the wall plug for your charger? Most hotel TVs have a USB connector on the back or side of the unit. All you have to do is connect your device to the TV with a USB cable and watch it charge up.

385

When searching for a hostel or hotel online, take a look at the three-star reviews. These tend to be the most honest and usually have both pros and cons about the place.

386

Want to extend the life of your rechargeable batteries? Put them in your hotel room's fridge. The cold temperatures will help them retain their charge when you're not using them.

387

Hotel curtains not closing all the way? Grab a pants or skirt hanger from the closet and use the clamps to fasten together the curtain panels.

388

Keep in mind that almost all hotels allow you to extend your checkout time by one hour. If you're at a busy business conference, this can often save you from waiting in a crowded checkout line.

389

Staying at a condo during your trip? Depending on the country that you're visiting, it's often cheaper (and more convenient) to pay the airline's extra suitcase fee and bring your own food.

390

Not enough counter surface in your hotel bathroom? Break out the ironing board for some extra space.

391

When you get to your destination, have your hotel receptionist or host write down the name, address, and phone number of the hotel in the country's native language.

392

Camping and forgot some of the necessary ingredients for making s'mores? Try this alternative: Twist open a cream-filled sandwich cookie (such as an Oreo) and add in some chocolate and a roasted marshmallow.

393

Hotel room too dry? You can make a simple DIY humidifier by wetting a towel, ringing it out so it's not soaking, and hanging it over the ironing board in front of the heating vent.

394

You can tell if a restaurant is authentic by which language is used for the sign and menu. If the majority of the menu items are in the restaurant's native language, then you'll probably get some delicious authentic food.

395

Having trouble falling asleep in your hotel room? It could be the room is too warm. The ideal temperature for sleeping is between 60°F to 62°F. If the hotel thermostat is not set to this, change it.

How to Override a Hotel Thermostat

396 Hold down the thermostat's "display" button.

397 Press the "off" button simultaneously.

398 Continue to hold down the "display" button, let go of the "off" button, and press the up arrow.

399 Release all of the buttons. You'll now have complete control of the thermostat.

400

Want to know the best spot to eat on a road trip? Look for the places where lots of trucks are parked. Most truckers have done the same routes hundreds of times, so they usually know where the best places are to eat.

401

Wondering if there are fresh sheets on the mattress in your hotel room? Look for crease lines. Hotels always tightly fold up their sheets after they've cleaned them. If there are creases, they're fresh.

402

If you're sleeping in a hostel with multiple people, always take the squeaky bed. You'll never get woken up by the bed's noises, as you'll be the one making them.

403

Can't find a sanitary surface to put your
toothbrush on at a hotel? Stab the handle
end through one of the paper coffee cups
that hotels provide for each room.

404

Got a hotel room without a fridge? Grab some ice and fill up the bathroom sink.

405

Don't leave a tip when you're in Argentina, France, Japan, Oman, or Yemen. Tips are usually included, and you'll actually risk insulting the staff by leaving one.

406

In general, when trying to find a good restaurant overseas, the smaller the menu, the better the food.

407

When checking in to a hotel in an area you don't know, grab the hotel's business card so you can show cab drivers the address.

408

PLANNING ON SLEEPING IN YOUR CAR? BRING ALONG AN INFLATABLE POOL RAFT AND THROW IT IN YOUR BACK SEAT FOR A LARGER BEDDING AREA. IN THE MORNING, YOU CAN JUST DEFLATE IT TO RESTORE SPACE IN THE BACK SEAT.

Chapter 8

MAXIMIZING YOUR VACATIONS

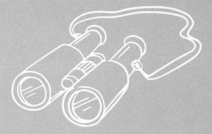

409

Want to visit Paris? You should know that there's an exact replica of the Eiffel Tower and other French architecture in Tianducheng, China, and staying there would be significantly less money than staying in Paris.

410

Backpacking with a friend? Swap backpacks while you're hiking or touring. If you need something from your backpack, you can just grab it without having to take the pack off your back.

411

Did you know that *Wikipedia* has a sister website for travelers? It's called *Wikivoyage*, a site where volunteer authors can write travel guides with tips and experiences about travel destinations and topics, and then others can edit it or add to it.

412

A lot of museums in New York are free. Some of them, like the American Museum of Natural History, have pay-what-you-wish admission fees, but bear in mind that these are just recommendations.

413

Looking to do some networking at a conference? Bring a power strip with some phone chargers. Not only is it an effective conversation starter; it also makes you look prepared and reliable. You'll have a bunch of new contacts in no time!

414

Some airlines have freebies for kids, like coloring pages, games, and activities to keep them entertained; just ask a member of the flight crew.

415

KEEP IN MIND THAT, WHEN YOU LOOK BACK ON VACATION PHOTOS TWENTY YEARS FROM NOW, IT WILL ALWAYS BE THE PHOTOS OF PEOPLE, NOT BUILDINGS, THAT YOU'LL LOVE THE MOST. SO FORGET TAKING THIRTY PICTURES OF THAT CASTLE AND INSTEAD TAKE A PHOTO OF YOUR FAMILY.

416

Want to go somewhere but don't have anyone to go with? Just go by yourself. It will be easy to meet a ton of people because you all have that band, sport, or event in common.

417

Looking for a unique view of a city that most people don't get? Find out where the tallest parking garages are, and go to their top floors.

418

A recent study showed that the best time to visit historical sites and landmarks is either very early, very late, or when people are eating (such as at lunchtime).

419

Going to Pompeii? Consider going to Herculaneum instead. Like Pompeii, it was also covered in ash and mud during the eruption of Mount Vesuvius in 79 A.D., but Herculaneum is better preserved. Plus, there will be far fewer tourists there.

420

If you or a family member is disabled, you can get a lifetime access pass to the National Park Service for free. The pass will get you and three adults into any national park in the United States at no charge.

421

Heading to the beach? Bring a fitted sheet and wrap the four corners on your bags, cooler, and so on to create a little wall and keep your area sand-free.

422

Always try to visit the local tourism office when you get to your destination. They know of all the special events coming up in the area, and may be able to give discounts on things you were already going to do.

423

Find out about city passes in your destination city. These passes offer a discount at many of the city's major tourist attractions. For example, in Paris, you can get a museum pass for more than sixty of the city's museums.

424

Planning a camping trip or going somewhere rural? Find out about any upcoming meteor showers and plan your trip around those dates. You'll never see meteor showers as vibrant as those that occur in the skies over rural areas—plus, it's free entertainment.

425

On a busy train or bus with a backpack? Flip it around to sit on your lap, against your chest. This will stop anyone from stealing from it, and it will give you some extra "personal space."

426

When visiting a famous landmark during your vacation, like the Eiffel Tower, make sure a person from your trip is in the photos. There's nothing worse than getting home and having a bunch of photos you could have found with a quick Google search.

427

Hate using public bathrooms but have no other choice? Choose the stall closest to the door, which has been shown to be the least used and therefore the cleanest stall.

Don't Do These Things in Public

428 **Chile:** Don't eat with your hands.

429 **China:** Don't give a clock or umbrella as a gift.

430 **Hungary:** Don't clink glasses when giving a toast.

431 **India:** Don't touch the opposite sex in public.

432 **Ireland:** Don't try to imitate an Irish accent.

433 **Norway:** Don't ask about going to church.

434 **Singapore:** Don't eat on public transit.

435 **Ukraine:** Don't give someone an even number of flowers.

436 **US:** Don't forget to give tips.

437

When in the UK, if the bar serves food but has no cutlery or napkins on the table, it means you have to get up and order from the bar.

438

Want local merchants to leave you alone? Wear headphones. You don't even have to listen to anything; just wearing them will make people less likely to bug you.

439

Hoping to get a genuine experience of a city? Turn off Google Maps and get lost on purpose. Casually strolling around a city is one of the best ways to really experience the culture and people of a community.

440

Before leaving for your vacation, do a quick Google search of your destination followed by the words "tourism scam." This isn't to scare you out of going but to increase your knowledge so you can enjoy your vacation.

441

If you ever get lost in a city, ask for directions from someone walking a dog—they are most likely from around the area.

442

Staying at an all-inclusive resort? Start your visit by giving the bartender a $20 tip. You'll get amazing service for the rest of your trip.

443

Spend your time having fun without having to search for a pharmacy: Always pack a first aid kit that contains things like stomach antacids, antibacterial cream, cold medication, throat drops, and, of course, bandages.

444

Looking to get a stunning view of the New York City skyline? Don't go to the Empire State Building—go to Rockefeller Center instead. The view is just as good, and there are hardly any lines to get to the observation deck.

445

Some souvenir shops (particularly in Mexico) are known to trigger expensive items to break when you touch them, forcing you to pay for damages. So, don't touch anything!

446

At the beach and don't have anyone around to watch your belongings? Bury them! Just stash your belongings in a plastic zip-top bag and bury them in the sand. Just make sure to leave yourself a marker in the sand so you remember where you left them!

447

Some hotels will let you take home their in-room coffee mugs. All you have to do is ask. In most cases, the hotel is glad to have you using a mug with their logo on it.

448

Traveling somewhere and want to learn the language? Start by figuring out their hundred most frequently used words. Those words make up about 50 percent of everyday speech.

449

WANT AN UPGRADE ON YOUR
PLANE, HOTEL, RESTAURANT,
AND SO ON? JUST ASK!
YOU'D BE SURPRISED AT
HOW HELPFUL SOME STAFF
ARE AND WHAT THEY'LL DO
FOR THEIR GUESTS. THEY
MAY EVEN OFFER YOU A
DISCOUNT. THE WORST
THING THAT COULD HAPPEN
IS THEY JUST SAY NO.

450

Fly into your cruise's port city the day before your cruise leaves. Sure, your cruise may not actually leave until 4 or 5 in the evening on your departure day, but what happens when your plane gets delayed and you are stuck in another city when your cruise is boarding? Go a day ahead and be ready.

451

If you're traveling to Canada, remember that they don't have pennies and therefore will round your change to the nearest five cents.

452

Going to the beach for the day? Bring some baby powder; it gets all that gunky wet sand off your hands and feet at the end of the day.

Meet Someone Special on Your Vacation? Here Are Some Dating Customs You May Want to Be Aware Of

453 **Australia:** The person who initiated the date is the one who pays.

454 **Brazil:** Public displays of affection are a desirable thing in a relationship.

455 **France:** A kiss while on a date is usually a symbol that you are now a couple.

456 **Iran:** It's against the law to go on dates.

457 **Japan:** Public displays of affection are not common or widely accepted.

458 **Korea:** Couples do not celebrate monthly or even yearly anniversaries.

459 **Mexico:** The man is always the one to ask out the woman.

460 **Netherlands:** It's just as common for a woman to ask out a man.

461 **Russia:** It's customary to bring a small gift like flowers to a date.

462 **Sweden:** People go on "potential dates" before "real" dates. "Potential dates" usually consist of going out for a coffee in the afternoon before proceeding to a "real" date.

463

Searching for ideas for a unique vacation in the future? Head somewhere rural on April 8, 2024—this is the next time a total eclipse will occur.

464

As a general rule, the more languages a restaurant has on its menu, the less authentic and more expensive the food will be.

465

Looking for something cheap to do in New York City? Go to a museum. Most of them are free, have "free hours," or allow you to get free tourist passes.

Chapter 9

STAYING SAFE
AND
HEALTHY

466

DO NOT travel anywhere if you have any signs of a fever, dry cough, or difficulty breathing/ shortness of breath. These are usually the first symptoms people experience with COVID-19.

467

One of the best ways to fight off jet lag is to go for a long run as close to your flight time as possible.

468

The first thing you should learn to say in another country's native language is any medical conditions you may have.

469

Avoid germs at the airport by applying to programs like TSA PreCheck or CLEAR. Once enrolled, you can use shorter security screening lines, and are not required to take off your jacket, shoes, and belt or put them in those germ-infested screening bins.

470

LOOKING TO AVOID PERSON-TO-PERSON CONTACT WHILE TRAVELING? BOOK DIRECT FLIGHTS. ALTHOUGH THE BEST DEALS USUALLY INVOLVE MULTIPLE LAYOVERS, YOU'LL AVOID A TON OF EXTRA EXPOSURE WHEN FLYING NONSTOP.

471

If a red line starts moving toward the center of your body from a bug bite, cut, or scratch, it's a serious sign that it's infected. Make sure you go see a doctor immediately!

472

Do you get sore teeth due to the high altitude of the airplane? It might not actually be your teeth, as this pain is often confused with a sinus problem. Try taking a sinus decongestant the next time this happens.

473

Looking to disinfect your seat before a long flight? Always make sure you're using sanitizer with at least 60 percent alcohol in it. Anything less won't get the job done.

474

You can boost your body's immune system while your diet and exercising habits are out of whack during travel by taking some echinacea.

475

Drying your hands with paper towels will reduce bacteria levels on your hands by 45–60 percent, while a hand dryer will increase levels by up to 255 percent because it blows around bacteria already living in the warm, moist bathroom environment.

476

Ten Natural Sleep Aids That Won't Make You Drowsy

- Ginkgo biloba
- Glycine
- L-theanine
- Lavender scent
- Magnesium
- Melatonin
- Passion flower
- Sleepytime tea
- Tryptophan
- Valerian root

477

One of the best ways to adjust to jet lag is to let your body get some sunlight when you get to your destination.

478

Statistically speaking, the check-in touch screens at airports have more germs on them than the toilet seats. Avoid these by checking in on your phone or at the check-in desk.

479

When checking in at a hotel, ask the front desk for a room that has been vacant for at least five days. This is the maximum amount of time some strains of COVID-19 can survive on surfaces.

480

Can't find any hand sanitizer locally? You can make your own by adding 75 ml of isopropyl alcohol, 10 ml of witch hazel, 15 ml of aloe vera, and 4 drops of tea tree essential oil into a spray bottle. Mix and spray.

481

Traveling somewhere with a questionable water supply? In some areas, people will reload bottles with regular water and pass it off as filtered water. To avoid this trap, drink seltzer water—it is harder to counterfeit.

482

Feel motion sick while traveling? The best thing to take is a motion sickness medication, such as Dramamine. If you don't have access to that, take an antihistamine, such as Benadryl, to relieve the symptoms.

483

If you have to go to an emergency room abroad, make sure to take your phone and a power cord. Because of COVID-19, most countries won't let friends or family into the ER with you, so this will be the only way to contact them with updates.

484

Before booking a flight, check out the airlines' policies on seating and boarding. During the COVID-19 pandemic, some airlines are blocking the middle seat, while others continue to fill to capacity.

485

Before getting in an Uber or Lyft, always check that the child safety lock (usually located on the inside surface of the vehicle's back door) isn't on.

486

Have a few too many drinks last night? Eat some honey on crackers. The fructose in the honey naturally accelerates the metabolism of alcohol in your body.

487

Bring a pair of disposable gloves to use only for cleaning things, and make sure to always wash your hands for at least twenty seconds after using them.

488

SITTING IN ONE SPOT CAN BE A REAL PAIN IN THE NECK. TRAVEL PILLOWS HELP, BUT SOMETIMES THE PAIN ISN'T COMING FROM YOUR NECK—IT'S COMING FROM YOUR BAD POSTURE. WHILE TRAVELING, MAKE A POINT OF CHECKING YOUR POSTURE AND DOING SOME STRETCHES EVERY HOUR OR SO.

489

Got a sunburn at the beach? A cup of tea can ease the pain. Brew up those free tea bags you get in the hotel room, leave the tea to cool, and then soak an old shirt or rag and place it over the sunburned area.

490

Before using hand sanitizer at the airport, make sure to check the expiration date. Most hand sanitizers start to become less effective at the two- to three-year-old mark.

491

If you're prone to getting motion sickness, bear in mind that the best place to sit on a plane is the middle seat, over the wing. This spot is known for being the least affected by turbulence.

492

Be aware that many public bathrooms are closed in response to COVID-19. Make sure to always use one before you leave for the day, and carry some sanitizing wipes or hand sanitizer with you at all times.

493

Know the COVID-19 numbers (and history) of a place before traveling anywhere. Just because your city is doing well and has precautions in place doesn't mean the city or country you're going to does. The best place to look up data is on the official government website for the country, city, or town.

494

Traveling to a highly polluted city? Make sure to bring glasses and several backup pairs of contact lenses. It's pretty common to get an eye or sinus infection after a week or two if you're constantly using the same contact lenses.

495

WANT TO AVOID TOUCHING
DOOR HANDLES? GET
YOURSELF A KOOTY KEY.
THESE ATTACH TO YOUR
KEY CHAIN AND LET YOU
OPEN DOORS AND PUSH
BUTTONS WITHOUT HAVING
TO TOUCH THEM.

496

Scared of getting mugged in a certain area?
Buy a cheap wallet and put a couple of dollars
in it. If you get mugged, hand over that wallet.

497

After it is applied, hand sanitizer will kill
germs for up to two minutes, so be sure
to apply before and after coming into
extended contact with shared surfaces.

498

Want to avoid picking up extra germs in your
hotel room? Wrap the ice bucket bag around
the TV remote for a DIY germ shield.

499

When at a hotel, take the stairs instead of
the elevator. You have no choice but to be
within 6 feet of someone in an elevator,
whereas the stairs give you a much better
chance to adhere to social distancing.

500

How to fix jet lag: Upon arriving at your destination, do not eat until 7 a.m. the next day (you can go a long time without eating and still be healthy). Force yourself to wake up at 7 a.m., open a window, stare at the sun, and then eat your first meal of the day. This helps correct your circadian rhythm, which is mostly affected by two things: sunlight and the timing of meals.

501

Try to avoid touching your face and eyes while traveling. This is one of the most common ways that germs can enter your system. If you have to sneeze, and you don't have a mask on, do it into your elbow.

502

Clean out an old stick of deodorant and stuff it with some extra cash and/or a backup credit card. Your money or cards are guaranteed to be safe because who steals sticks of deodorant?

503

When flying, increase your social distancing radius by booking a window seat. If you think of an imaginary 6-foot circle around you, having a wall on one side cuts the radius in half.

504

Don't use your debit card while on vacation. Instead, use your credit card. If your credit card is stolen, you are not liable for the unauthorized purchases made on that card. If your debit card is stolen, there is often no way to recover the money.

505

One of the safest places to be while traveling during COVID-19 is inside the plane. Modern aircrafts change their cabin air twenty to thirty times per hour, which removes more than 99 percent of airborne particles. So, the more time you spend in the airplane, the better.

Ten Things You Can Do to Instantly Improve Your Health

506   **Take some vitamin C:** Whether it's a pill or lozenge, getting some vitamin C in your system can help boost your metabolism.

507   **Drink water:** When you feel like you need something but can't figure out what it is, drink water. It's always water.

508   **Wash your hands:** One little germ can multiply into more than eight million by the end of the day. Don't let them.

509   **Walk:** You'd be surprised how much exercise you can get by making it a point to walk places. Even when you're on the plane, don't be afraid to take a couple of strolls down the aisle.

510   **Stretch:** Always start and end your day with a quick five- to ten-minute stretch. This will make you feel more refreshed in the mornings and help you fall asleep more quickly.

511 **Meditate:** Never hesitate to take a five- to ten-minute break from whatever you're doing to calm your mind and relax.

512 **Breathe:** Much like meditating, doing some breathing exercises can help you relax and refocus. Take a deep breath, hold it for five to seven seconds, and exhale.

513 **Eat some fruit:** Make sure you're including some fruit in your diet. Grocery stores all around the world sell fruit, so you can grab some no matter where you go.

514 **Use hand sanitizer:** Most hand sanitizers kill 99.9 percent of germs and are usually sold in airport convenience stores.

515 **Call your mom:** Simply giving your mom a call and hearing her voice has health benefits similar to a getting a hug, and has been proven to help reduce stress levels.

516

Don't want COVID-19 to ruin your summer vacation? There are many other alternatives, like camping or renting an RV, that offer little to no person-to-person contact.

517

The average gas pump has 11,000 times more germs on it than a toilet seat. Keep disinfectant wipes in your vehicle to wipe down pump handles and sanitize your hands before pumping gas.

518

To limit your time near people in airport lines, have your boarding pass ready, be mindful of what's allowed on the plane, and keep your liquids and electronics in easily accessible places.

519

Worried about getting your money stolen? You can easily hide some money for a little backup stash in a hollowed-out lip balm tube.

520

Use the old paper towel trick when entering and exiting the airplane bathroom. Simply wrap a paper towel or toilet paper around your hand so you don't have to touch the handle.

521

If you're planning on staying in some hostels, make sure to bring flip-flops to wear in the showers. With the high traffic these places get, you'll be glad you brought some self-defense.

522

Want to feel safer in your hotel room? You can buy a travel door alarm online for under $20. The portable device hangs on the doorknob and is equipped with two metal sensors that slide between the door and the doorframe.

523

Pack disinfectant wipes to use at your hotel. When you arrive, wipe down the door handles, light switches, TV remote control, telephone, and coffee pot.

524

Did you know there are no regulations about how often airlines have to wash their pillows and blankets? It's true. So just to be safe, make sure to bring your own.

525

You can avoid the germs at the airport by simply driving to your destination. You can easily drive to many domestic locations in roughly the same or less time that it takes to fly, once you factor in time spent traveling to and from the airport, the flight itself, and waiting in lines.

526

Don't have a face mask handy? You can make one by placing two layers of cotton sheets around your mouth and nose and securing the sheets with an elastic band.

527

When booking a hotel, try and make it a walkable distance from your destination and local attractions. You'll avoid public transit and limit person-to-person contact.

528

Due to the low humidity in airplanes, it's very common for your nose and mouth to dry out, making you more susceptible to viruses and bacteria. So while onboard, make sure you're drinking more water than you usually would.

Chapter 10

COMMUNICATION AND TECHNOLOGY

529

911 isn't a universal number. When you're abroad and need to reach a country's emergency service line, simply dial 112. No SIM card is needed for this either.

530

If you're in an area where you should have cell phone service but don't, put your phone on airplane mode and then switch back. This will cause your phone to register and find all the towers in your vicinity.

531

Download the Google Translate app before you leave. Its camera feature lets you point it at things like menus, posters, and street signs, and translates for you in real time.

532

Going to the beach? Put your phone in
a zip-top sandwich bag, and you'll still
be able to use the touch screen!

533

The GPS app on your phone will work while
you're on the plane. This is a fun way to track
your location, your speed, and your arrival time.

534

Looking for a power outlet on a plane,
train, or bus? Check under the seats.
Several modes of transportation in other
countries hide them under there.

535

Need to access free Wi-Fi? The best places to go are
Starbucks, Taco Bell, Arby's, Subway, McDonald's,
Best Buy, Burger King, Lowe's, and Target.

536

Want your own digital tour guide? The Wikipedia app has a location feature that shows you historical, cultural, institutional, and geographical landmarks nearby; plus, it takes you to the *Wikipedia* page for them.

537

Looking for some authentic cuisine while traveling? Try the Eatwith app. It offers unique dining experiences, tours, and even classes taught by locals.

538

TripAdvisor has maps you can download to your phone that have a built-in compass function. This will help you navigate old, organically developed towns like Rome or Paris, as well as find foreign street names that are difficult to recognize.

539

KEEP IN MIND THAT GOOGLE
CALENDAR (AND SOME
OTHER CALENDAR APPS)
AUTOMATICALLY ADJUSTS TO
YOUR CURRENT TIME ZONE.
MAKE SURE YOU'RE AWARE
OF THIS FEATURE, WHICH,
ALTHOUGH IT IS CONVENIENT,
CAN ALSO CAUSE PROBLEMS.

540

If you ever need some free Wi-Fi at the airport, just add "?.jpg" at the end of any URL. This will bypass the paywall of a majority of Wi-Fi networks.

541

Did you know that most airlines have a representative who monitors their *Twitter* account twenty-four hours a day? If you have a problem with your flight, reaching out for help to the airline via *Twitter* can actually be a much quicker option than standing in a long line or waiting on hold.

542

Can't figure out a Wi-Fi password? A lot of restaurants and stores set their phone numbers as their passwords. Don't know their phone number? If you have Google Maps cached for the area, it can give you their number.

543

The universal word for the bathroom (except in North America) is "water closet." If you type "WC" in your phone or write it on a piece of paper, you're likely to be pointed in the right direction.

544

Have a bad habit of speeding? Use the Waze app. It functions as a personal GPS and also has an audio warning to alert you when you are going over the speed limit.

545

Need to make some calls to the office while overseas? Use Google Voice. It's completely free to use, and it even works with office landlines!

546

Don't want to risk using your phone where you don't have a plan? The iPhone Reminders app can notify you when you've reached a specific location.

547

Need to go to the bathroom all of a sudden? Use the Flushd app to find the nearest bathrooms along with user-based ratings and reviews.

548

There's an app called TraffickCam that lets you help combat human sex trafficking by simply uploading photos of the hotel rooms you stay in. This database is used to find and then prosecute traffickers by matching the photos they post of their victims to your photos.

549

Need to keep track of your expenses on a business trip? Use the Shoeboxed app. It's an easy way to track your receipts, generate expense reports, and get reimbursed. You can even use it to track your mileage.

550

DON'T WANT TO PAY FOR BOOKS AT THE AIRPORT? USE *BOOKCROSSING* (HTTPS:// BOOKCROSSING.COM), A WEBSITE WHERE TRAVELERS AND LOCALS RELEASE THEIR BOOKS "INTO THE WILD" BY LEAVING THEM AT COFFEE SHOPS, PARKS, AND EVEN AIRPORTS SO THAT OTHERS CAN READ THEM TOO.

551

Most phones allow you to check Google Maps and use the GPS offline. It's a smart way to save money and data from your travel plan while overseas.

552

How to get free Wi-Fi at airports: Go to the airport's opening web page (where they offer the Wi-Fi plans), open up their "marketplace" (where you can shop with their partners), and click on any link to another site (which could be a product/review/company's page). Then use this new tab to browse the Internet for free (just make sure you keep the previous tabs open).

553

If you're a student traveling abroad, you can get easy, secure, and free Wi-Fi spots by signing up with eduroam. They have zones in more than one hundred different territories—plus it's free!

554

If your phone battery is dangerously low and you need it for later, don't turn it off now and back on later. Doing so will waste more battery life. Instead, set it to airplane mode and leave it on.

555

Phone battery low while using GPS? Take a screenshot of the list of directions and view it as a photo. It takes much less battery to view a photo than to run a GPS app.

556

Almost every airport convenience store has a phrase book you can pick up to learn the most common words of that country's language.

557

Getting a bunch of business cards at your conference? Instead of cramming all of them in your wallet, take pictures of them.

558

How to get free Internet on US flights for a short period of time: When you are prompted to download a video player for in-flight entertainment, access to the Internet is granted to your device. This is usually for only about ten minutes, but it's enough time to check some emails and send a couple text messages for free!

559

Hate traveling without your standing desk? Set up your laptop on your hotel room's ironing board. It's the perfect height!

560

Make sure to always pack a power strip or extension cable for your electronics. Finding free power outlets in hostels or airports can sometimes seem impossible.

561

How to use Photoshop to delete random tourists from your photos:

- Set up a tripod where you want to take the photo.
- Snap fifteen to twenty shots over the course of two minutes.
- Open all the images in Adobe Photoshop by selecting File/Scripts/Statistics and then choose "median."
- Photoshop will automatically find what's different in the photos (the random tourists) and remove it.

562

Need the Wi-Fi password to a restaurant, hotel, and so on? Check out that business's listing on *Foursquare*. The comments will usually contain its Wi-Fi password.

563

Before booking a seat on an airline, input your flight number onto *SeatGuru*. This website and app will show you the seat map for your plane and the best seat(s) to select.

564

Don't want to pay hotels for Wi-Fi or use their slow Internet? Pack a mini travel Wi-Fi router and plug it into an Ethernet port (usually under the TV). You'll now have your own personal Wi-Fi connection.

565

Make sure you have Viber, WhatsApp, or Skype downloaded onto your phone before you leave. These applications will let you phone, video call, text, or instant message for free.

566

Looking for a good spot to snap a photo? Check out the hashtags of your location on *Instagram* and sift through the photos to find the right place.

567

Need a quick way to communicate in another language? Point to these thirty-two icons accordingly to get your message across. Take a picture of this page for reference.

568

In a hotel room where the power is controlled by inserting your room key into a slot? You should know that these key card slots can work with any card in them. This will give your room power so that you can keep the air conditioning on while you're out, and it'll prevent you from leaving without your key card.

569

Need to find Wi-Fi quickly? Make sure you have the WiFi Map app downloaded onto your phone. It shows you a map of nearby Wi-Fi hotspots and their passwords (and no, the app doesn't need Wi-Fi to run).

570

Always take a picture of your ID or contact info as the last photo on your digital camera just in case you lose your SD card.

571

Forget to bring your phone charger? Ask the front desk at your hotel if they have any in their lost and found bin. This is one of the most common things left behind by guests.

572

Want to make sure you have Wi-Fi on your next business trip? Before you book your hotel, check its Wi-Fi status at *Hotel WiFi Test*.

573

Want to know exactly how much something costs in your destination's local currency? Download the XE Currency app. It lists virtually every currency with real-time rates.

574

Always learn to say hello and thank you in the native language of the country you're visiting.

How to Say "Hello" in Thirty Different Languages

575 **Bosnian:** *zdravo* (ZDRAH-voh) / *merhaba* (MEHR-hah-bah)

576 **Bulgarian:** *zdravejte* (zdrah-VEY-teh)

577 **Chinese:** *nǐ hǎo* (nee haow)

578 **Croatian:** *bok* (bohk)

579 **Czech:** *ahoj* (ahoy)

580 **Danish:** *hallo* (ha-loh)

581 **Dutch:** *hallo* (HAH-low)

582 **Estonian:** *tere* (TEHR-reh)

583 **Finnish:** *terve* (TEHR-veh)

584 **French:** *bonjour* (bohn-ZHOOR)

585 **German:** *guten tag* (goo-ten tahk)

586 **Greek:** *yasass* (YAH-sahss)

587 **Hindi:** *namaste* (nuh-muh-steh)

588 **Hungarian:** *szervusz* (SEHR-voos)

589 Icelandic: *halló* (ha-loh)

590 Indonesian: *halo* (hah-loh)

591 Irish: *dia duit* (JEE-ah GHWIT)

592 Italian: *salve* (SAHL-veh)

593 Japanese: *konnichiwa* (kohn-nee-chee-wah)

594 Korean: *annyeonghaseyo* (an-nyee-ong-hah-seh-yo)

595 Mongolian: *sain baina uu* (sain bai-na OO)

596 Norwegian: *god dag* (goo dahg)

597 Polish: *cześć* (cheshch)

598 Portuguese: *olá* (oh-LAH)

599 Russian: *zdravstvuyte* (ZDRAHST-vooy-tyeh)

600 Spanish: *hola* (oh-lah)

601 Swedish: *hej* (heh)

602 Thai: *sà-wàt-dee* (sah-wah-dee) followed by *khrap* (for men) or *khaa* (for women)

603 Tibetan: *tashi delek* (tah-shee del-ek)

604 Vietnamese: *xin chào* (sin chow)

Chapter 11

HEADING HOME

605

Heading home but lost your ID? You can actually fly without one. Arrive at the airport an hour earlier than usual, and you'll be put through an examination process to prove your identity. This only works for domestic flights.

606

Don't want your stinky vacation shoes to smell up your suitcase on the way home? Pack them in hotel shower caps.

607

Bringing home a bottle of wine from your travels? Protect the bottle from breaking by placing one boot or shoe over the top and one over the bottom before putting it in your suitcase.

608

If you're heading home during the winter and find that your car's lock is frozen, squirt some hand sanitizer in it, and it will unfreeze almost instantly.

609

Want to remember your trip? Make a new soundtrack for each place you visit. Now whenever you want to relive your vacation just listen to that soundtrack.

610

Find an awesome radio station abroad but can't get it back home? You can access any public radio station around the world at the Radio Garden app.

611

Leaving a country and still have some extra currency? Consider giving it to a homeless person or to a server as one last good tip, as it will most likely go unused when you bring it back home.

612

KEEP YOUR SUITCASE FRESH
FOR YOUR NEXT TRIP BY
THROWING IN A FEW DRY
TEA BAGS WHEN YOU GET
HOME. THIS WILL ABSORB
ALL OF THOSE UNPLEASANT
ODORS FROM YOUR TRAVELS.

613

Planning on going on the same cruise again?
Book your trip before leaving the ship. Companies
frequently offer a few hundred dollars of onboard
credit if you book another trip while you're there.

614

Feeling down about being home? Try re-creating
your favorite meal from your vacation. Food
and memory are intricately tied, so you'll feel
like you're right back in vacation mode.

615

Leave a buffer of a few days before going
back to work. This makes the transition
easier, and you can take the time to unpack,
relax, and still be in vacation mode.

616

Bring a souvenir or picture from your vacation to place on your desk at work. Souvenirs remind you of the fun you had and can help ease any stress you have at work about the transition back.

617

Have a bunch of leftover foreign currency? Stop by a Starbucks and load it onto a gift card; it automatically converts the foreign currency to your local currency at an above-average exchange rate.

618

Friend picking you up at the airport? Sometimes it's much easier to use the free shuttle services to get out of the busy arrival terminal and get picked up at another location.

619

If you're the kind of person who brings back souvenirs for everyone, buy one extra general gift that can work for someone you may have forgotten about.

620

Not every souvenir has to cost money. Try gifting people evocative photos, sand/ seashells, ticket stubs, or maps that you brought back from your trip.

621

Returning home and have bus/train passes that are still good for a little bit? Abide by the circle of passes and hand them over to someone else traveling there. Someday it may come back to you.

Ten Things to Do on the Last Day of Your Vacation

622 Make sure everything you're bringing home fits in your suitcase.

623 Charge up all your electronic devices.

624 Dry your wet clothes. If you have a wet bathing suit or workout clothes, this can put you over the maximum weight allowance.

625 Change your watch back to local time.

626 Sort out your in-flight entertainment. Chances are you're taking the same airline home, so you know what to expect.

627 Make sure you have your house and car keys for when you get home.

628 Confirm your transportation home from the airport.

629 Cash in your leftover currency (or put it on a gift card).

630 Make sure you have all your travel documents (passport, work visas, ID, and so on).

631 Relax. You're still on vacation, even if it's your last day there.

632

Want to remember your vacation? Try out
a new perfume or cologne during your trip.
Since smell is one of the strongest triggers
of memory, every time you sniff this scent,
it will bring back those memories.

633

When you are back home and putting away
important documents, like your passport,
immunization records, work visa, and so on,
always return them to the original spot where
you found them. This will most likely be the first
place you look for them again in the future.

634

Too lazy to unpack after your trip? Dump all your
clothes out onto your bed. Want to go to sleep?
Now you're forced to put away your clothes first.

635

Before returning home from your trip, see if you can get someone from work to email you an update on what you've missed. This will make things easier when you're transitioning back into work life.

636

Although it's never fun returning from vacation, it's the perfect time to create new dietary habits. Take advantage of the fact that your body isn't really used to any kind of habitual patterns at that moment.

637

Never throw out your packing list! Use it as a reference guide by adding and subtracting from it to make an ultimate packing list for the future.

638

Looking to relive your vacation at home?
Buy a diffuser with some oils from the part
of the world you were in. Smell is one of
the best ways to spark your memory.

639

One of the best ways to get back to your regular
routine is to write a to-do list. Converting thoughts
in your head into a tangible list can really help
spark some drive and is proven to relieve stress.

640

Want to keep that vacation tan for longer?
Eat plenty of meat and dairy products
when you return. This increases your body's
production of melanin, the compound that
can help you stay tan in the winter months.

641

When you get home, one of the most effective methods of getting back to normal is to drink 8 ounces of water for every hour you were on your flight.

642

Avoid posting pictures of your vacation on social media until about a week after you return home. Posting your trip while you're away is like giving thieves an invitation to your empty house.

643

Get back to feeling like your normal self with a detox bath: Mix 2 cups Epsom salt, ¼ cup grated ginger, and a few drops of eucalyptus oil and add to a hot bath (as hot as you can stand).

644

LOOKING FOR A WAY TO
BRING HOME SOUVENIRS
OR GIFTS FOR PEOPLE
WITHOUT BREAKING THE
BANK? TRY SHOPPING IN A
LOCAL THRIFT STORE BEFORE
YOU LEAVE. THE ITEMS ARE
USUALLY MUCH CHEAPER,
MORE AUTHENTIC, AND NOT
GEARED TOWARD TOURISTS.

645

Finding it hard to focus on work after a vacation? Start a few emails, memos, and so on before you leave for your trip, but don't finish them. It's a lot easier to get back into the work mindset when you've already technically started the thought process.

646

Save all of your shopping on a cruise ship until the last day. Most of the shops like to clear their inventory at the end of a voyage, so you'll often get some megadeals then.

647

Studies have shown that we need at least a couple of months to make or break a habit. Use this figure as a guide when you come home to get back on track with your diet, sleep, exercise, and so on.

648

Feeling nostalgic for your vacation? Try printing out your photos and making an album. This will help you relive all the happy moments and provide some closure on your trip.

649

Now that you're back, be sure to check your credit card and bank statements to make sure there is no suspicious activity. You've just been sharing your credit card number with merchants in other places; it's always good to check for security.

650

Struggling to get back to the gym after a vacation? Just do some stretching, get a massage, or relax in the sauna at the gym. Just the fact that you make the trip there helps start a habitual pattern that makes it easier to visit the gym in the future.

651

Want to get over those postvacation blues?
Start planning your next vacation. It's hard to
be bummed about being home when you're
already excited about your next journey.

INDEX

IMPROVE YOUR LIFE—
ONE HACK AT A TIME!

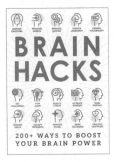